Prince Hal
and his friend
Jack Falstaff

Shakespeare's Henry IV Part 1
Retold with music by Alan Oberman
Illustrated by Robin Carter

For Moya, Saoirse and Nia
with all my love
A.O.

First published in the United Kingdom in 2014
by Cambria Books
Carmarthenshire
Wales
United Kingdom
www.cambriabooks.co.uk

ISBN 978-0-9576791-9-1

Text and illustrations © Alan Oberman 2014
Music © Alan Oberman 2014

The rights of Alan Oberman to be identified as the author and composer of this work have been asserted by him in accordance with the Copyright, Designs and Patents Act 1988.

All rights reserved
Unauthorised public performance, broadcasting and copying of these CDs are prohibited.

A CIP catalogue record for this book is available from the British Library.
Produced by Shore Books and Design
Blackborough End, Norfolk PE32 1SF

Prince Hal and his friend Jack Falstaff

CD 1 (inside front cover)
Track 1   The story with music (42 minutes)
Track 2   The story without music (26 minutes)

CD 2 (inside back cover)
Incidental Music: the story told through music (20 minutes)

Narration: Philip Bowen
The musicians:
Piano   Laura Greenwood
Violin   John Hymas
Saxophone   Alan Oberman
Electric bass and guitar Graeme Lamble
Drums   Tony Egan
Vocals   Lu Mason
Flugelhorn   Simon Fraser

Engineered and edited by: Robin Lamble

Thanks to: Delyth Cresswell (for the words to 'Tyrd Yma Cariad')

Recorded at: The Institute, Llangamach Wells, Wales and Penlanole, Rhyader, Wales.

~ Sir Jack Falstaff ~

Prince Hal and his friend Jack Falstaff

Let me tell you a story, the story of Prince Hal and his friend Jack Falstaff. It was once told in a strange and beautiful language by William Shakespeare. As the story proceeds, we will hear some of Shakespeare's words.

A prince ought to behave in a prince-like way: taking an interest in running the country and learning how to fight like a soldier. But Prince Hal much preferred having fun with his mates. Hal's favourite friend was Jack Falstaff, not a person you would expect the Prince to choose as a friend. For a start, he was old, older even than Prince Hal's father. And he had a bird's nest of a beard and an enormous beer-belly from drinking lots of sherry. But, Jack Falstaff was the sunshine at the party; when he was there it came alive, like fireworks, and when he wasn't, it was all a bit dull. He would say what nobody else dared to, like calling the Chancellor of the Exchequer 'fart face'. And when Jack Falstaff spoke, everybody listened. Prince Hal was brought up at the Palace where people were serious and well-behaved. Jack Falstaff gave Prince Hal freedom. He was free to have fun, free to be naughty.

Prince Hal went to look for Jack Falstaff. Where would he find him? In the pub of course. When Hal got there, everyone was drinking and dancing and having a great time. On seeing Prince Hal, they all shouted 'hurrah!' and Hal joined in with the dancing. Jack Falstaff was much too much of a lump to jump about, but he too got on his feet and danced in time to the music. Prince Hal grabbed hold of Jack Falstaff and, while everyone cheered, made him dance round and round the pub.

Exhausted, Jack Falstaff flopped into a chair and called for, 'More sherry!' One of Prince Hal's mates was a young man called Ned Poins. He was useful to the Prince because he would do whatever the Prince told him to do. Ned Poins could run fast and wrestle and was quick with a dagger which made him dangerous.

Jack Falstaff said to Ned Poins, 'I've heard there are rich traders taking money to London tomorrow morning, is it true? Shall we rob them? Come on Hal, you'll join us won't you?'

At first, Prince Hal refused, 'Who, I rob? I a thief? Not I, by my faith.' But Ned Poins had an idea to play a joke on Jack Falstaff and whispered in Prince Hal's ear, 'Now, my good sweet honey-lord, ride with me tomorrow. I have a joke that I cannot manage alone.'

Early in the morning when all was quiet, Falstaff was hiding in the woods with three mates waiting for the traders. Prince Hal and Ned Poins were also hiding but not where Jack Falstaff could see them. Four traders walked slowly down the hill. They had taken woollen cloth to Rochester and sold it there, and now they were on their way back to London. Their horses were carrying the money bags.

Suddenly, Jack Falstaff jumped out, waving his sword and shouting, 'Strike, down with them, cut the villains' throats! Ah, whoreson caterpillars, bacon-fed knaves.' The traders were very frightened and soon let themselves be tied up.

Falstaff was just dividing up the money with his mates when …

Prince Hal and Ned Poins, with masks covering their faces, rushed out, shouting and waving their swords. Jack Falstaff was so scared, he ran away as fast as he could.

Why did Prince Hal do this to his friend? Because he wanted to hear what Jack Falstaff would say in the pub that evening. When they were there, Prince Hal said, 'What's the matter, Jack?'

'We stole a thousand pounds this morning and it was all taken from us. Sixteen of them attacked us four, but I never fought better in my life.'

Everybody in the pub was listening. Only Prince Hal and Ned Poins knew that Jack Falstaff was lying, that it wasn't sixteen who had attacked him but just the Prince and Ned Poins.

Prince Hal said, 'Sixteen really? Pray God you have not murdered some of them.'

'I killed two of them. Two, I am sure, Hal. If I tell thee a lie, spit in my face, call me horse. I went at them with my sword like this, and this, and this, and four of them...'

'What, four? You just said you'd killed two of them.'

'These four came at me but I stopped all seven swords with my shield.'

'Seven? Why there were only four just now.'

'Are you listening, Hal? I thrust my sword like this and quick as a thought I finished off seven of the eleven.'

'You fought with eleven men and killed seven of them. O monstrous! Eleven men grown out of two. These lies are as fat as the man who made them. We two, Ned Poins and I, saw you four attack the four traders. Then we jumped out on you and you ran away as fast as you could roaring for mercy. Now, what have you got to say for yourself?'

Everybody listened to see if Jack Falstaff could wriggle out from his lies. For a moment, Jack Falstaff was at a loss for words then he said, 'Of course, I knew it was you, I just pretended I didn't know you. Should I have killed the son of the King?' Everybody laughed.

Suddenly, there was a knocking on the door. It was a messenger from Prince Hal's father, King Henry. Prince Hal must go straight to see him in the morning.

'Now you're in trouble lad,' Jack Falstaff said. 'When you see your father, you'd better know what you're going to say.'

Then Hal said, 'Tell you what, why don't we rehearse it. You pretend to be my father and question me.'

They put a wooden stool on the table and helped Jack Falstaff climb up and sit on it. This was his throne. They put a cushion on his head. This was his crown. Everybody in the pub became quiet as they listened to what Jack Falstaff would say as he pretended to be the King.

'Hal,' said Jack Falstaff, putting on a king-like voice, 'I'm amazed at where you spend your time and who you hang around with, all those dropouts and scumbags and cheats. It pains me to have to speak to you like this. You shouldn't have anything to do with that lot.

'But there is one man often seen with you who's different to the others. He's a good man. I don't know his name.'

Hal said, 'What sort of man, your Majesty?'

'Well now, he's quite big, with a cheerful look, very dignified, a true knight, age, about fifty or so. Ah, now I remember his name, it's...'

And everybody in the pub shouted out, 'Falstaff!' and fell about laughing.

Jack Falstaff said, 'That man Falstaff, he's really honest. You stick with him, but all those others, have nothing to do with them.'

Prince Hal said, 'You get down off the table and pretend to be me. I'll get up there and I'll be the King.' Prince Hal put the cushion on his head. Again everyone became quiet as they waited to hear what Prince Hal would say.

Making his voice like the King, Prince Hal said, 'Hal, my boy, the complaints I've had about you are shocking. Why do you go around with that old fat barrel of a man, that dustbin of disease, that lord of lies, that lumbering ox? What's he good for except drinking and cheating and eating? What's he good at, apart from nothing?'

'I don't know who your Grace is talking about,' said Jack Falstaff.

'That white-bearded, leader of layabouts...'

And everybody called out, 'Falstaff'.

Jack Falstaff said, 'I do know the man and there's no wrong in him.

'My good lord, chuck out Poins, chuck out all these other rascals, but for sweet Jack Falstaff, kind Jack Falstaff, true Jack Falstaff, valiant Jack Falstaff, don't banish him from friendship with Prince Hal. If you banish plump Jack Falstaff, you banish all the world.'

'I do,' said Prince Hal, 'I will.'

The next morning, cap in hand, Prince Hal came to see his dad, King Henry. Hal knew he was in for a telling off.

'You're a disgrace,' said King Henry, 'we've given up on you. The hope and expectation of thy time is ruin'd.'

But then the King said, 'You've no idea what troubles there are in this land. I don't know why I'm telling you this, for as much as you'd care, but my enemies are creating an army in Wales to march against me and make someone else king. And I wouldn't be surprised if you joined them.'

Prince Hal had expected the dressing down but he was stung by this last accusation.

'Do not think so, you shall not find it so; and God forgive them that so much have sway'd your Majesty's good thoughts away from me! I will redeem all this and in the closing of some glorious day be bold to tell you that I am your son.'

The King softened. This is what he wanted to hear. He said, 'I'll set off to march to Wales to meet the rebel army. You go and round up more soldiers and join me later.'

Meanwhile, in the pub, Jack Falstaff was feeling very fed up. All this talk of war! And then, the landlady of the pub told him he had to settle his bill.

'I'll not pay a penny,' said Jack Falstaff, 'there are thieves in this pub have robbed me of money and a very expensive gold ring from off my finger.'

'I know you Sir Jack,' said the landlady, 'you're just trying to wriggle out from paying your bill. And I've heard the Prince many a time say that ring was copper not gold and not worth a farthing.'

'The Prince is a snotbag,' said Jack Falstaff 'and if he were here and said that, I'd smash his head in.'

Just at that moment who should walk into the pub but…Prince Hal himself! With barely a heart-beat pause, Jack Falstaff said, 'How now, lad? What's up? Are we all off to war? This pub is a bawdy house. They pick pockets. They pinched a gold ring off my finger while I slept.'

'That ring,' said Prince Hal, 'was not worth a penny.'

'That's what I told him you'd said, my Lord,' said the landlady, 'and he said he'd smash your head in if you said so. Tis true as I am an honest woman.'

'You're as honest as a stewed prune,' said Jack Falstaff.

Then Prince Hal said to Jack Falstaff, 'Well I do say the ring was copper and not worth a ha'penny. Do you dare to keep your word and have a go at me now?'

'Well Hal, if you were simply a man, I would dare, but seeing as how you are a prince, I fear thee as I would fear the roaring of a lion cub. But tell me, are the police after me about the robbery of the traders?'

'I am your good angel, I have paid back all the money.'

'Uggh! I don't like the idea of paying back money.'

Then Prince Hal told Jack Falstaff that they must all go to fight a rebel army. 'You will be in charge of a company of soldiers, but first you have to go and round them up and get them ready to fight.'

When Prince Hal had left, Jack Falstaff muttered, 'I'd rather stay in this pub.'

Far, far away from King Henry's palace, deep in the heart of Wales, was a mighty castle. This was the home of Owain Glyndwr, Lord of Wales.

People said Owain Glyndwr had magical powers. That when he was born, the earth shook. That by pointing his finger, he could start a fire. That he could see in the dark. That he could command the wind and the rain and bring on a storm.

Owain Glyndwr had a beautiful daughter called Catrin. One day, Owain Glyndwr captured a noble lord called Edmund Mortimer and held him prisoner in his castle. Edmund Mortimer was no ordinary prisoner. Many great lords thought that Edmund Mortimer should be King of England instead of King Henry. At first Owain Glyndwr thought he could ransom Edmund Mortimer, get the English lords to pay him heaps of money to send Edmund Mortimer back to them. But when Edmund Mortimer saw the beautiful Catrin, he fell in love with her. The trouble was, she could speak Welsh but could speak no English and he could speak English but could speak no Welsh.

Owain Glyndwr told Catrin that Edmund Mortimer wanted to marry her and he said that if they were married, he would fight King Henry and help Edmund become King of England. They did marry and lived with Owain Glyndwr in the castle in Wales.

Then, late one afternoon, there came to the castle a young man riding a magnificent horse and leading a large number of soldiers. With banners flying and drums beating, the soldiers marched into the castle. That young man was Hotspur, the most famous warrior in all of England. He could take on four swordsmen at the same time and beat them all. Hotspur was always in the front when leading his soldiers into battle. He was praised for his courage and respected for his skill. Hotspur was a powerful lord from the north of England. He had once helped King Henry become king. But now he thought King Henry was far too big for his boots. He had heard the news that Owain Glyndwr and Edmund Mortimer were making plans to attack King Henry and he had come to offer his support in making Edmund the King of England instead of King Henry. Owain Glyndwr warmly welcomed his new guest.

In the great hall there was a roaring fire. They had eaten well when Owain Glyndwr called for his musicians to play for them. 'And those musicians that shall play to you, hang in the air a thousand leagues from hence, and straight they shall be here: sit and attend.' The musicians played for them.

Catrin spoke loving words in Welsh to her husband, Edmund Mortimer, but he could not understand. Owain Glyndwr translated her words. 'She bids you on the wanton rushes lay you down, and rest your gentle head upon her lap, and she will sing the song that pleaseth you, and on your eyelids crown the god of sleep, charming your blood with pleasing heaviness.' Catrin sang:

> Tyrd yma cariad, gorffwys dy ben yn fynghol. Paid ti a'm gadael paid a mynd i'r gad, heb imi ddyfal gyda thi.

Which means, 'Come here my darling, rest your head in my lap, don't leave me, don't go off to war unless you take me with you.'

Having rested a few days, Hotspur was impatient and anxious to lead his soldiers to face King Henry and his army. Owain Glyndwr and Edmund Mortimer weren't ready so Hotspur set off without them. Owain Glyndwr and Edmund Mortimer went to recruit more soldiers and would catch up with Hotspur as soon as they could.

Meanwhile, Jack Falstaff was very pleased with himself. He had been given money to recruit a hundred and fifty soldiers. First, he went to all the better off people where he lived and commanded them to join the army. He knew they would rather do anything than fight in the army. So, with a nod and a wink, he let them know that if they paid him, he would let them off. Then, he made all those who couldn't pay him become his soldiers. Unemployed old men, ex-prisoners, young lads, poor peasants who looked after sheep and goats and pigs, all were forced into Jack Falstaff's troop of soldiers. When he had got a hundred and fifty men and boys together, they set off on the march to Wales to join King Henry's army.

On the way to Wales, Prince Hal saw Jack Falstaff marching. 'Tell me, Jack, whose men are these here?'

'Mine, Hal, mine.'

'I never did see such pitiful rascals. They're so thin and unfit to fight.'

'Tut, tut, good enough for cannon fodder, they'll fill a grave as well as any better man.'

Hotpsur had set up his camp near Shrewsbury town. He got word that Edmund Mortimer and Owain Glyndwr were on their way but delayed and would be days before arriving. Hotspur was a very brave soldier but at times somewhat reckless. He decided to go into battle without the support of Owen Glyndwr and Edmund Mortimer. King Henry was camped a mile away. The two armies settled down to sleep for the night. Tomorrow the battle would begin. Who knows who would be killed and who would survive? Who knows who would win, who would lose?

Early next morning, the two armies formed up in ranks facing each other: the archers with their great longbows, the foot soldiers with pikes and daggers and the knights in armour on horseback with mace and swords. Given the word, they began moving forward, towards each other.

First to attack were the archers, letting loose a hail of deadly arrows. Many men were cut down even before they came to the enemy. Then the shock as the armies met and the chaos of fighting men: stabbing, slashing, kicking, screaming. Horses fell; men wounded or dead or dying lay in the mud. And still the battle raged on. Kill, kill or be killed. 'Is Hotspur alive?' 'Yes, yes fight on.' 'Is the King dead?' 'No, no, there he is, fight on.'

King Henry was surrounded by enemy soldiers and in grave danger. Prince Hal fought his way to the side of the King and rescued him. 'I see now, you are a true son to me,' said the King. 'But you are wounded, you must leave the battlefield.'

'Not I,' said Prince Hal, 'I must find Hotspur and challenge him to fight.'

Jack Falstaff was also in the fight, but rather than get hurt he lay down on the ground and pretended to be dead. Jack Falstaff thought to himself as he lay on the mud, there's no honour in pretending to be dead. But can honour fix an arm that's cut off? Can honour take away the pain of a wound? What is honour? A word. What is that word, honour? Air. And if you win honour in dying, can you feel it when you're dead? No. Can you hear it? No. It's useless then. I'd rather do without honour and stay alive.

Falstaff heard two men having a horrific fight. They were determined to kill each other. He half opened one eye. It was Hotspur and Prince Hal. They were both brilliant at sword fighting and the fight went on and on until suddenly, Hotspur made a mistake and received a fatal blow from Prince Hal's sword and he fell to the ground and soon died.

Prince Hal said, 'Here lies a great soldier. When he was alive, a kingdom was too small a place for him; but now two paces of the vilest earth is room enough.'

Prince Hal turned and saw Jack Falstaff dead on the ground. 'What, my old friend? Could not all this flesh keep in a little life? Poor Jack, farewell! I'll see to it that you are properly buried soon.'

When Prince Hal had gone, Jack Falstaff opened his eyes and said, 'I'd rather not be buried.' He got up and stared at Hotspur. 'Even though he's dead, I'm scared of him. Supposing he's pretending to be dead like I did. I know what, to make sure, I'll stick my sword in him and swear it was me that killed him and then they're sure to reward me.'

With Hotspur dead, King Henry's army soon won the battle.

When Prince Hal saw Jack Falstaff carrying the dead Hotspur on his back, he could not believe his eyes. 'Art thou alive? Or is it fantasy that plays upon our eyesight. I prithee speak, we will not trust our eyes without our ears.'

Falstaff threw down Hotspur's body. 'For this, I think your father should make me an earl or a duke.'

'But I killed Hotspur myself and saw you dead.'

'Did you? Lord, lord, how this world is given to lying! I grant you I was down, and out of breath, and so was he, but we both got up in an instant and fought for at least an hour. I gave him this wound in the thigh there and if there's any man would deny it I'll make him eat a piece of my sword.'

Prince Hal knew that Jack Falstaff was lying but said, 'You are the strangest man. But if telling a lie will do you some good, then, for now, I'll do it.'

Hotspur was dead and his army defeated. Every soldier in King Henry's army cheered Prince Hal as a champion. King Henry said, 'You are truly my son.'

This battle was over, but they couldn't rest for long; Edmund Mortimer and Owen Glyndwr were on the march and there would have to be another battle. But that's another story. And Jack Falstaff? Well, for now, he was in everybody's good books. But how long will that last?

Prince Hal and his friend Jack Falstaff
The Story told in Music

00:00	King Henry (piano) is worried about a plot against him led by Hotspur (violin).	07:23	Falstaff is fed up: all this talk of war and the landlady of the pub wants to be paid.
00:53	In the pub, there is music and dancing.	07:53	Owain Glyndwr's Castle.
01:16	Jack Falstaff (bass) is drinking in the pub.	09:01	Hotspur arrives at the castle.
01:48	Jack Falstaff dances to the pub music.	09:26	Catrin and Edmund fall in love.
02:08	Prince Hal (saxophone) arrives at the pub.	11:19	The musicians play.
02:40	Prince Hal dances to the pub music.	12:04	Catrin sings, 'Tyrd Yma Cariad'.
02:56	Prince Hal with Jack Falstaff.	13:25	King Henry is marching to Wales.
03:13	Prince Hal and Jack Falstaff dance to the pub music.	14:09	Jack Falstaff is leading a dismal bunch of soldiers to Wales.
03:49	Dawn, the traders walk their horses down the hill through the wood.	14:23	Prince Hal is marching to Wales.
04:43	Jack Falstaff and three mates attack the traders.	14:39	Hotspur leads an army to meet King Henry.
05:18	Prince Hal and Ned Poins jump out on Jack Falstaff and he runs away.	15:03	The two armies sleep.
05:35	In the pub that evening.	15:47	The armies advance towards each other.
05:54	Prince Hal exposes Jack Falstaff's lies.	16:09	The armies join in battle.
06:11	A messenger from King Henry arrives.	16:33	Jack Falstaff pretends to be dead.
06:23	Jack Falstaff pretends to be the King.	17:15	Hotspur and many others are killed.
06:39	Prince Hal pretends to be the King.	17:53	Prince Hal emerges from the battlefield.
07:05	After getting Prince Hal's promise of support, King Henry sets off to march to Wales to meet the plot against him.	18:58	Prince Hal is cheered as a hero.
		19:32	Jack Falstaff has the last word.